Options Trading

Fundamental Skills To Dominate Options Trading

by
Jordon Skyes

☐ Copyright 2016 by Jordon Sykes - All rights reserved.

This document is geared towards providing exact and reliable information in regards to the topic and issue covered. The publication is sold on the idea that the publisher is not required to render an accounting, officially permitted, or otherwise, qualified services. If advice is necessary, legal or professional, a practiced individual in the profession should be ordered.

- From a Declaration of Principles which was accepted and approved equally by a Committee of the American Bar Association and a Committee of Publishers and Associations.

In no way is it legal to reproduce, duplicate, or transmit any part of this document by either electronic means or in printed format. Recording of this publication is strictly prohibited and any storage of this document is not allowed unless with written permission from the publisher. All rights reserved.

The information provided herein is stated to be truthful and consistent, in that any liability, in terms of inattention or otherwise, by any usage or abuse of any policies, processes, or directions contained within is the solitary and utter responsibility of the recipient reader. Under no circumstances will any legal responsibility or blame be held against the publisher for any reparation, damages, or monetary loss due to the information herein, either directly or indirectly.

Respective authors own all copyrights not held by the publisher.

The information herein is offered for informational purposes solely and is universal as so. The presentation of the information is without a contract or any type of guarantee assurance.

The trademarks that are used are without any consent, and the publication of the trademark is without permission or backing by the trademark owner. All trademarks and brands within this book are for clarifying purposes only and are the owned by the owners themselves, not affiliated with this document.

TABLE OF CONTENTS

Introduction

Chapter 1: Brief Introduction to Options Trading

Chapter 2: Skill #1 Options TradingTerminologies

Chapter 3: Skill #2 Reading Options Table

Chapter 4: Skill #3 Analyzing Options

Chapter 5: Skill #4 Option Strategies

Conclusion

Jordon Sykes

Jordon Sykes

INTRODUCTION

I want to thank you and congratulate you for downloading the book, *"Fundamental Skills to dominate Options Trading"*.

This book contains fundamentals of Options trading, as well as powerful steps and strategies of Options Trading that are quintessential for becoming successful in this field.

Starting from the basics, this book also explains various complex strategies and concepts pertaining to Options Trading in a simple, easy to follow. Supported with ample illustrations, charts, and examples, this book is guaranteed to make you well versed in the fundamental skills requiredforOptions Trading.

Within these pages, you will find

- Precisely what a Options means and where to trade them
- Why you should trade options,
- Important Terms and fundamental concepts of Options trading
- What are put options ?

- What are call options ?
- How to analyze options
- Various Optionstrading strategies for making money

And lots more...

Remember, people spend THOUSANDS of dollars on seminars and courses to learn even a tenth of what is being disclosed in this book. Equipped with the knowledge gained from this book, your overall outlook towards Options trading is guaranteed to becomea positive one! If you wish to dominate Options Trading by having a thorough understanding of all the Fundamental Skills, we have got it covered!

Thanks again for downloading this book, I hope you enjoy it!

CHAPTER 1: BRIEF INTRODUCTION TO OPTIONS TRADING

"Options Trading? Man, heard that is a tough one to crack!"

"I tried my hand at options trading at the urging of my friend. But I lost so much money in a single day, I quit the whole thing!"

"Options Trading? Never heard of it. What *is* that thing?"

When asked about Options Trading, these were some of the responsesI received frompeople. It was disheartening to see blank stares or outright negative reactions about one of the best ways to make fast money!

This got me thinking. So, I sat down andanalyzed why the very mention of Options Trading elicited such hostile responses and traced it down to two basic things – ignorance and fear.

People are either (i) genuinely ignorant of the very existence of Options Trading, or (ii) harbor so much fear about losing money by doing Options Trading that they simply avoid the whole thing like ebola.

Here's a fact – Options Trading is one of THE most profitableways to trade if it is done right. Remember what I said about ignorance and fear earlier? There is a solution to overcome them both – it is by gaining enough knowledge about the subject.

This book is a powerful tool for gaining insight about Options Trading in a simple, easy to follow, and *interesting* manner. This is intended to be a one-stop reference for gaining the fundamentalskillsrequired to become successful in Options Trading.

By the end of this book, I guarantee that you and Options Trading would be on *very* friendly terms!

However, let me be upfront – Options *are*complex and would need to be understood well before you can start profiting from them.

That said, there are four basic fundamental skills required to become a highly successful Options Trader. They are

1. Good Knowledge about the variousOptions Trading terminologies

2. FamiliaritywithOptions Table and understanding on how to read an options table

3. Knowledge to perform Options Analysis using

    a. Technical Analysis

    b. Open interest

    c. Option greeks and volatility

    d. Put Call ratio

4. Knowledge about important options strategies

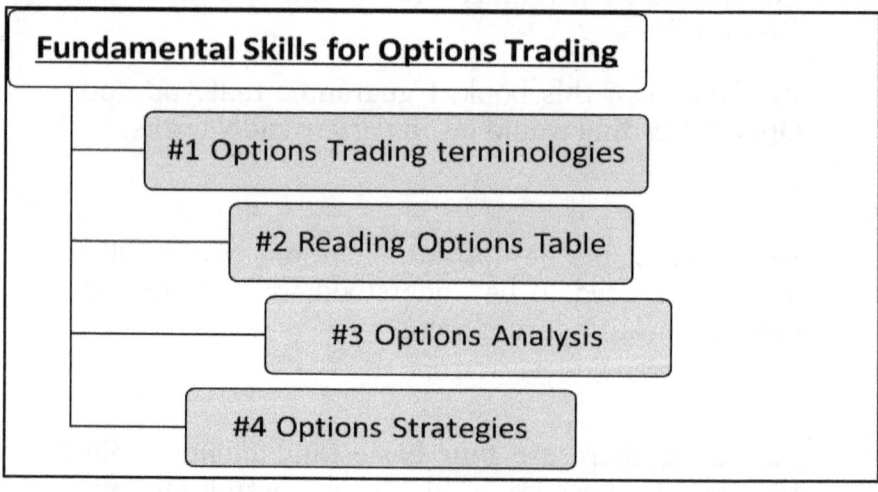

Before moving onto the first fundamental skill, here are some basic pertinent information regarding options trading.

Where are Options Offered?

Prior to 1973, the trading of options was unregulated. They were allowed to be traded over the counter. Now, listed options are allowed to be traded only on regulated exchanges. These must adhere to SECrules for trading.

Following are the major option exchanges in U.S.A - American Stock Exchange (AMEX), Chicago Board of Trade (CBOT), Chicago Board Options Exchange (CBOE), Chicago Mercantile Exchange, International Securities Exchange (ISE), New York Stock Exchange (NYSE), Pacific Stock Exchange (PSE), and Philadelphia Stock Exchange (PHLX).

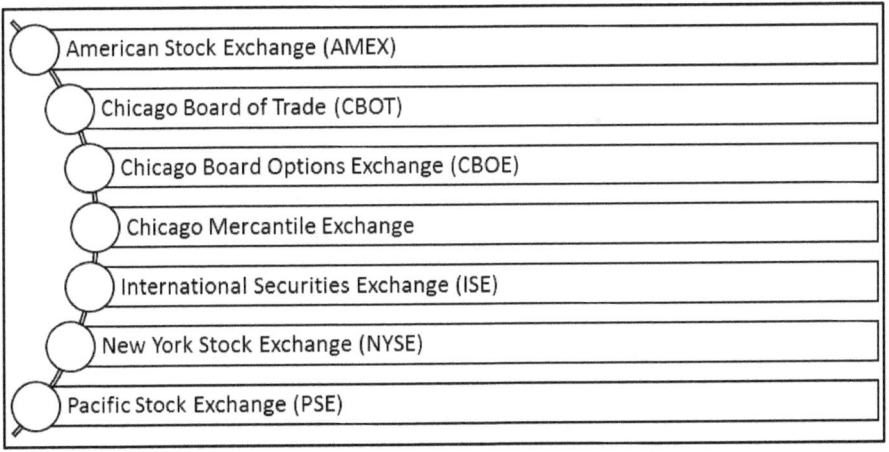

What are the Similarities and difference between stocks and Options?

Following are the similarities as well as differences between stocks and options.

Similarities	Differences
• Options are securities, just like stocks. • Options also trade on exchanges regulated by SEC • Options can be traded like securities and the orders are transacted through retail participants and market makers using buy bids and sell offers.	• There is an expiration date for Options while the stocks can be held for as long as you like. • Options are held electronically and do not have certifications like the stocks. • The number of options that can be traded on a specific underlying stock is limitless, unlike stocks. • Options do not give dividends or voting rights like stocks.

Why Options?

Options can be chiefly used in two ways - to hedge as well as to speculate. It can also be used as an income-boosting strategy.

Speculation: speculation can be defined as a ***bet or a prediction on the security's movement.*** Options can be used for making profits when the market moves up or down or even sideways.Speculation is a slightly risky aspect of options as you should be highly accurate about the direction of the move, magnitude of the move, as well as the timing of the move.

You should be able to predict if

- the stock would move up or down,
- how much price would be increased or decreased, as well as
- how long it would take.

Despite the risks, speculation is highly profitable due to the use of ***leverage***.Leverage is basically committing only a percentage of the capital required for the trade and borrowing the rest.Thus, just a single options contract can be used for controlling 100 shares. Hence, even a slight movement in the expected direction would result in significant profits without needing to invest a substantial amount of money.

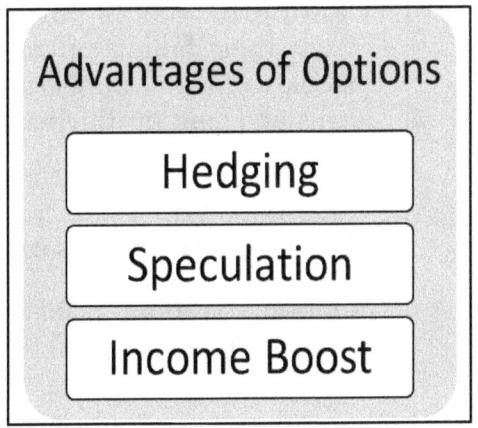

Hedging: Options can also be used as a risk management tool, for **protecting the investor portfolio against a decrease in stock price**. This is called as hedging. In simple terms, hedge is basically like an insurance policy against a downturn of the investments.

If your stock has gained you substantial profits that are yet unrealized, you can use options as a hedge. For doing this, you can purchase puts for the stocks. In case the stock price rises, the option would expire worthless. But the increase in price would offset the premium costs. Alternatively, in case the stock price decreases, you can sell the put at a profit and cover the losses to your portfolio.

Income boost: Options can also be used for boosting income. If you are anticipating a market downturn, you can purchase puts onstocks to profit from their falling prices.If you expect a particular stock to have a bullish bias, you can also purchase calls and gain profits from them.

What are the Risks of Options Trading?

Options Trading is also rife with inherent risks, depending on how you trade it.

If you are an options holder, your risk is limited to the premium paid for the options.

On the other hand, the risk is substantially higher in case you are an options writer, especially if you write an uncovered call. The loss would be directly proportional to the increase in the stock price.

When using leverage, it would be wise to remember that it works as a two-edged sword – even though it gives ahigher percentage of return, the corresponding loss percentage would also be high.

Options also have the risk of time decay. This means that the option value decreases as you approach the expiration date. Hence options are also called as wasting assets as they are worthless after a specific date.

Option holders are not entitled to rights typically bestowed to shareholders like dividends and voting rights.

Now that you have a basic idea about where options are traded, its advantages as well as disadvantages, it is time to move onto the first Fundamental skill required for dominating Options trading - Knowledge about the various Options Trading terminologies.

Chapter 2: Skill #1 Options

Trading Terminologies

A good understanding about the various Options Trading terminologies is a pivotal fundamental skill required to become successful in Options Trading. In fact, they form the very foundation of Options Trading.

Let us start with the obvious.

What is an Option?

An option is basically

- A binding **contract** between a **buyer** and a **seller** (also called as a **writer**) and has strictly defined terms as well as properties.

- An option is a **security** similar to a stock or bond.

- Options are a type of **derivative instrument** as the price of an option is derived from the underlying stock.

- Options are traded in **units** called as **contracts**.

- Options can be European style or American style based on the permission to exercise the option before the expiration date.
    - ***American-style options***: here the option buyer can exercise the option at <u>any time</u> before the expiration date.
    - ***European-style options***: here the option buyer cannot exercise the option before the expiration date.
- It typically represents ***100 shares*** of underlying stock for American Options.
- Options give buyer the ***right*** (but ***not*** an ***obligation***) to
    - buy or sell some ***underlying instrument***
    - at a ***specified price*** (called ***strike*** price)
    - on or before a certain ***expiration date***.
- On the flips side, an Options seller will have an ***obligation*** to buy or sell the stocks if the buyer wishes to exercise before the expiration date.
- There are ***two types*** of option contracts – ***puts and calls***.
    - A ***call*** is an option to BUY.
    - A ***put*** is an option to SELL.

The concept of Call and Put Options can be simplified and explained using the below table:

TYPE of Options contract	Call	Put
Buyer (Holder)	Right to Buy	Right to Sell
Seller (Writer)	Obligation to Sell	Obligation to Buy

Underlying instrument

Underlying instrument, also called as underlying interestcan be a

- stock
- exchange traded fund (ETF)
- commodity
- futures contract
- foreign currency or
- stock index

Strike price

The strike price is the price that is specified in the option contract at which the underlyinginstrument is **bought or sold**in case the option is exercised.

Expiration Date

The **expiration date** is the date after which the option contract ceases to exist. In case an option is notexercised on or before to the expiration date, all the right contained in the option contract becomes invalid. Usually, the last day to buy, sell, or exercise options is the **third Friday** of theexpiration month for monthly options. There are also weekly options available.

Another important term is whether the option is In the Money and Out of the Money. So, what do they mean?

A **_Call option_** is called as

- **In-the-money (ITM)** ifthe underlyingstock's current market value is **above** the exercise price of the option

- **Out-of-the-money (OTM)** if the stock's current market value is **below** the exercise price.

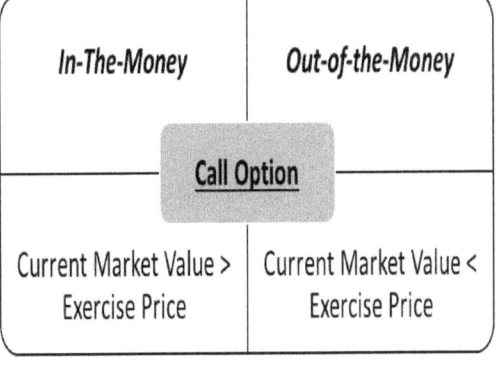

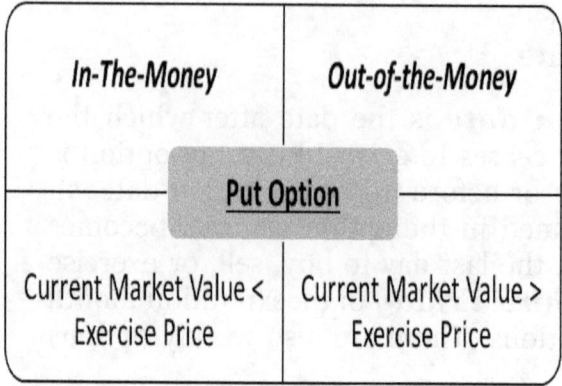

A **_Put Option_** is called as

- **In-the-money** if the underlying stock's current market value is **below** the exercise price of the option
- **Out-of-the-money** if the stock's current market value is **above** the exercise price.

An option is considered to be worthless if it is not in-the-money at expiration.

There is also something called as **At The Money (ATM)**, wherein the Exercise Price (Strike Price) is at the same level as Current market value.

i.e, Exercise price = current market value

How do options give huge returns?

So, how exactly do options give you huge benefits? It is best explained using a simple example.

Let the amount available for investment for Adam and Brian be $1000.

Assume that the stock ABC has a high probability of an upward move according to research reports. Let us say that the shares of ABC sell for $10 a share.

Adam decides to invest the $1000 for ownership of stock ABC. This means that Adam buys 100 shares of company ABC stock at $10 each, investing a total of $1,000.

Hence, $10 X 100 = $1000 investment in ownership of stock ABC.

On the other hand, Brian invests the same $1,000 in options.

Assume that he buys 20 calls, each at the cost of $50, at a strike price of $12.50.

Basically, he spends $0.50 per share of ABC or $50 per 100 shares (1 contract).

Hence $50 X 20 contracts = $1000 investment in options.

Now, assume that the stock ABC moved up by $5 after purchase. This means that the cost per share is now $15 for the stock ABC. Let us now assume that both Adam and Brian decide to take profits and exit their trades.

When Adam sells his 100 shares at $15, he would get $1500. Subtracting the invested amount, he makes a profit of $1500- $1000 = $500. This $500 is a 50% return on his investment (ROI).

Now, for Brian, it's a slightly different scenario. When the stock price moves to $15, his $12.50 strike option would be *in-the-money* by $2.50. Consequently, the value of his call would now be increased from the earlier $0.50 per share to at least $2.50 per share. This would mean that each contract would give him $250 when he sells them.

On exiting all 20 contracts, he would get $5000. ($250 X20 = $5000).

Subtracting the invested amount, he makes a profit of $5000- $1000 = $4000. This $4000 is a massive 400% return on his investment.

	Initial investment amount	Profit when there is $5 move upward	ROI
Adam (Ownership)	$1000	$500	50%
Brian (Options)	$1000	$4000	400%

But wait, there is more to the story.

Assume that 100 shares of a stock XYZ were purchased for $40 by Rachel. This means that she spent $4000 for ownership of the stock XYZ.

At the same time, assume that Amelie purchased two contracts of the options of the same stock XYZ for $200 premium.

Now, if the stock price decreases by $5, Rachel would have a loss of $5 X 200 = $1000. On the other hand, Amelie's losses would be limited to just the $200 premium that was paid during the purchase of the call option!

Next, let us understand what a Premium means.

Premium

Premium is the ***price you pay*** for when you ***buy*** an option. Similarly, thepremium is the ***price you receive*** when you ***sell*** an option.

There is no set price for premium, it changes from day to day. Typically, for options expiring in the current month, the premium would be higher if the option is currently in-the-money.

On ***buying*** options (puts or calls), you will have a ***net debit*** initially. This is because you have spent money that might never be recovered back unless you exercise your option or sell it at a profit. The final profit gained would be the total profit minus the amount paid as premium.

On ***selling*** options(puts or calls), you will have a ***net credit*** initially. This is because you would collect the premium. If the options are never exercised, you will simply keep the premium as the profit. However, if the options get exercised, you should sell or buy the underlying stock on the exercised price, and can also keep the earlier premium.

An option's premium has two parts:

- Intrinsic value
- Time value

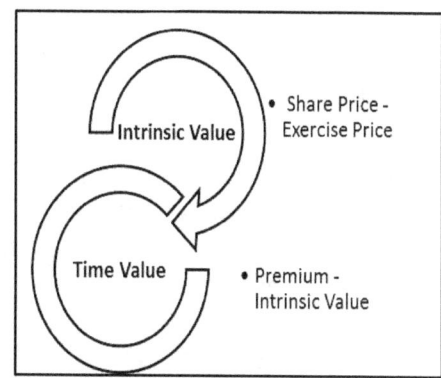

Intrinsic value is the price by which the option is in-the-money. This is basically the exercise price subtracted from the market price of the share. Note that Out-of-the-money and at-the-moneyoptions have no intrinsic value.

Time value is the difference between the premium and theintrinsic value. This means that the longer the amount of time for market conditions to work to yourbenefit, the bigger the time value.

For example, let the stock 'XYZ' have a share market price of $30, premium of $6, and an exercise price of $25. Then, intrinsic value = $30 -$25 = $5. Time value = $6 - $5 = $1

Let us now move on to take a closer look at the important terms and definitions of Options Trading.

Option Greeks

Option Greeks are nothing but the **forces** that collectively and independently **affect the premium** of the options. Assessing the changes in premium is one of the most important skills that an option trader needs to have and hence it is important to have a basic knowledge of the various Greeks. The option Greeks affect the options on a real time basis and they affect each other as well. Although this sounds a little complicated, it is not so.

The various Greeks are Delta, Gamma, Theta, and Vega. Here's a brief overview about the four greeks.

Delta – The Delta measures the rate at which the premium of the option changes with respect to the movement of the underlying stock

Gamma – The Gamma measures the rate at which the Delta moves

Theta – The theta measures the impact on the premium based on the number of days left for expiry

Vega- The Vega measures the rate at which the premium of the option changes with respect to the change in volatility

This is best represented using the below chart.

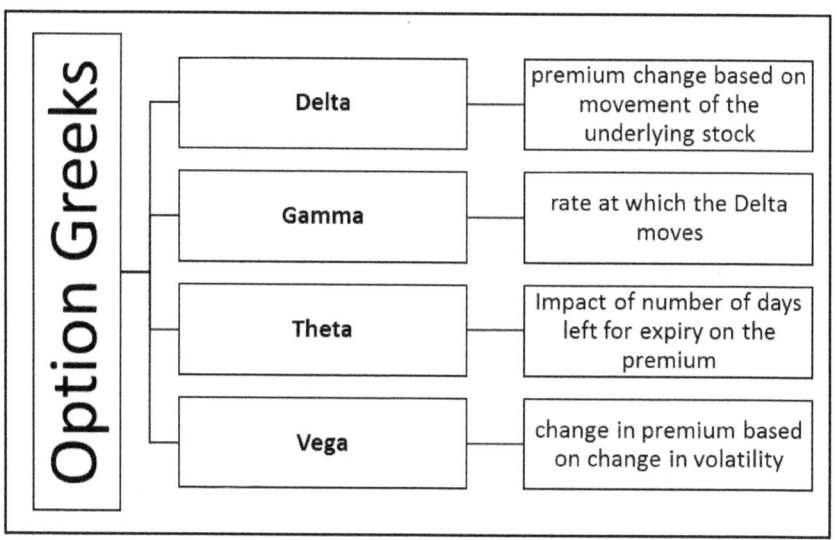

Let us take a look at each of these forces one by one. Let us first try to understand the delta.

#1 Delta

The Delta measures the rate at which the premium of options at various strike prices changes with respect to the price change of the underlying stock.

- The Delta is calculated using the Black-Scholes model.
- The value of the delta is between
    - 0 and 1 for a **call** option and
    - -1 and 0 for a **put** option.

- The **closer** the **price of a stock and the strike price**, the **higher** would be the **delta**. So the ITM options would be having the highest delta i.e. close to 1.

This is best understood using an example.

Let us assume that the stock ABC was trading at $1000. Now let us assume that the call option at the strike price of 1100 was trading at $5. Please note that each call option at every strike price would have a delta associated with it. So now let us assume that the delta of the call option at strike 1100 is 0.5.

This essentially means that with every $1 movement in the price of the stock ABC, the call option at strike 1100 moves by 50 cents. Using this information, we would be able to calculate the price of the call option, with respect to the change in theprice of the underlying.

Now let us say the price of the stock went up by $20, we can calculate the price of the call option at astrike of 1100 as follows.

$20 * 0.5 = $10

So the new price of the call option at strike of 1100 would be calculated as

$5 + $10 = $ 15

Similarly, the value of a put option can also be calculated.

For the same stock ABC, let's assume that the put option of strike 900 was trading at $7. Also, let's assume the delta of the 900 put was -0.4. Now suppose the stock of ABC went down by $20, then we can calculate the price of the put option at strike 900 as follows.

$20 * 0.4 = $8

So, the new price of the put option of strike 900 would be

$7 + $8 = $ 15.

The delta is **particularly useful when we have to choose between two options**. Let us understand this with an example.

Assume that a stock is trading at $ 100 and you have to choose between the call option of strike price of 105 and 110.

Let's say the delta of the call option with a strike of 105 is 0.5 and the delta of the call option with astrike of 110 is 0.3.

This means the former would move 50 cents with every $1 increase in theprice of the underlying stock while the latter would move only 30 cents with every $1 increase in theprice of the underlying stock. So, as we can see the first strike price (105) would be a better option.

But then again this also would depend on the days left for the option to expire. If the expiry of the option is far away, then it might make sense to buy the option of strike price 110 as there is a more realistic chance of the option reaching there.

So, it is better to buy 'In the money' and 'At the money' options if the expire is nearby.

It makes sense to buy an OTM or 'Out of the money' option only if the expiry is far away.

Also in the case of an OTM option, the delta keeps increasing as the option turns into an ITM or ATM option.

The delta of a call option ranges from 0 to 1. The further the strike price is away from the price of the underlying, the closer it would be to 0. Similarly, the delta of a put option ranges from -1 to 0.

A few key points to remember about Delta are as follows

1. The delta changes with the change in theprice of the underlying.
2. The delta would be closer to zero for OTM options
3. The delta would be 0.5 for ATM options.
4. The delta would be closer to 1 for ITM options.
5. Delta can be used to choose the strike price.

#2 Gamma

Gamma calculates the rate at which the delta changes with respect to the change in the underlying.

Unlike Delta, Gamma would be a positive number for both calls and puts. We would not be going into the calculation part of Gamma as it is beyond the scope of this book.

However, let us look at one practical use of Gamma. Gamma can be used for determining the risk associated while buying or selling an option.

Gamma determines the rate at which the delta changes. This means that if the delta changes at a faster rate, so would the premium of the option.

Hence, it would be better to avoid shorting options which have a large gamma.

Also, there would be a delta expansion as the option moves from ATM to ITM. The gamma would be high in this case. It is better to avoid shorting such options.

Delta does not change rapidly for ITM or OTM options. Out of the money options are the ideal candidates for shorting (writing an option).

Thus, we can see Gamma is quite useful in determining the risk associated with each option. In short,

- Look for options with **low Gamma while selling**
- Look for options with **high Gamma** while looking to **buy** an option.

#3 Theta

The third Greek that we would look into is the Theta. Theta is also calculated using the Black-Scholes formula. Before we get into theta, let us once again revisit the time factor of an option premium.

Every option has a time premium associated with it and this keeps decreasing and becomes zero on the day the option expires.

For example, lets us assume that there is a month to go before the option of stock ABC expires.

Let's say the underlying stock is trading at $100 and the current value of the call option of strike price 95 is $7. As we saw earlier, the option price is made up of twocomponents, the intrinsic value, and the time premium.

In this case, the intrinsic value is $5 and $2 is the time premium as there is still a month to go for the expiry of the option. The time premium keeps reducing as the expiry approaches.

Now let us consider another example. The call option value of strike 105 is $ 2. Since 105 is above the current price of the underlying (100), the $2 is the time premium and the intrinsic value is 0.

So, in short, option premium = intrinsic value + time premium.

Coming back to the time component or Theta, it is nothing but the rate at which an option loses its time premium as the time passes.

The time premium reduces on a daily basis and ***theta is useful for calculating the rate at which the time premium loses value***.

Theta would always be a positive number. Theta is a useful indicator for option sellers. At the beginning of a series, options would have a high time premium and hence are sold by option sellers.

As the expiry of the option gets closer, the time premium reduces but the theta or the rate at which it loses premium increases. So even though the premiums might be less, it is safer to write or sell options when the expiry is near.

#4 Volatility (Vega)

The fourth Greek that we would be looking into is the Vega. It calculates the rate at which an option would lose value with change in volatility. The volatility is calculated using Standard Deviation but we are not going into the calculation part here.

There are various websites that would give the volatility of an option.

The daily volatility of a stock is useful for placing the stop loss for a particular trade.

When the volatility is high, selling options is a better option rather than buying it. This is because the premiums of options increase when the volatility increases. Similarly, when the volatility is low, buying strategies should be considered.

There are basically three types of volatility.

1. ***Historical*** volatility: This is calculated using the closing price of the underlying stock over a period of time
2. ***Forecasted*** volatility: This is calculated using various forecasting models.
3. ***Implied*** volatility: This is the most important one and is basically based on the expectations of the market.

Volatility smile

The Volatility smile is plotted with the implied Volatility on the y-axis and the strike price on the x-axis. As we can see the ATM or the 'At the money' options have the lowest implied Volatility. Whereas the Out of the money options and the 'In the money' options have the maximum implied volatility.

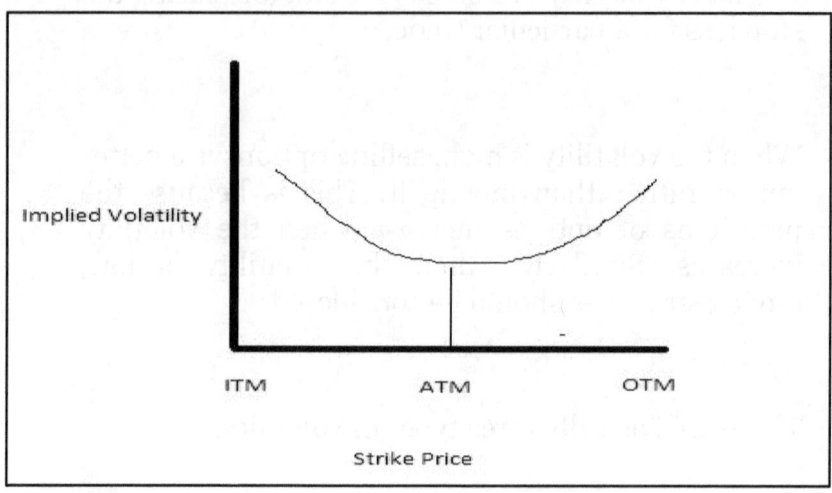

So, based on this it is a good idea to write or sell OTM options when the volatility is high. Volatility is a useful indicator that helps us to decide whether to buy or sell options at any given point of time.

- It is generally better to **buy options when the volatility is low** and is expected to increase. The option premiums would be low when the volatility is low and would increase when the volatility increases.
- Similarly, it is better to **sell options when the volatility is high** and is expected to reduce. This is because as a seller we would

like to pocket high premiums and want the premium to reduce as the volatility reduces.

Professionaloptions traders generally sell options before important economic events, quarterly results etc. to take advantage of the high volatility. But do note that the volatility alone should not be used for making this decision. The time left for an expiry should always be considered when deciding to buy or sell an option.

In conclusion, it is important to have a basic understanding of the various option Greeks as it helps us in

- Choosing the right strike price.
- Determining whether to go for ITM, OTM or ATM options at a given point of time
- To decide if it's the right time to buy or sell an option

The various option Greeks are freely available on several websites. The option Greeks are also usually provided by the broker and are usually available at the trading terminal. They can also be calculated using the options Greeks calculator.

Option calculators are again freely available and would calculate the Greeks once you provide a series of inputs like the strike price or the exercise price, the expiration date, the volatility (which is the annualized volatility of the underlying stock), the interest rate (the risk-free interest rate of the country in which the underlying stock is listed) and the yield rate (the yield rate as a percentage, of the country in which the underlying stock is listed).

Let us now move onto some more key terms of Options Trading

Open interest

Open interest is basically the number of open positions for an options series. It can also be defined as the number of open contracts in the current market. When open interest is high, it means that there are many open positions on that specific option. This need not necessarily indicate bullishness or bearishness.

Volume

The sum total of opening, as well as closing contracts that were traded over a specific period of time, is called as volume. For example, if an option has a high daily volume, it means that many investors opened or closed positions on that option for that given day.

Liquidity

Liquidity basically indicates the demand for a particular options series. If there are more number of buyers and sellers in the market, it indicates a greater value of liquidity for that options series. Higher liquidity is an indication of higher demand for a particular option. This can work either way. It can result in anincreasein the premium if there are lots of buyers, or decrease of the premium in case there arelots of sellers.

Bid

Bid is the highest price that the floor trader is willing to buy (to bid). When placing a market order, Bid is the price at which you would sell.

Ask

Ask is the lowest price that the floor trader is willing to sell (to ask). When placing a market order, Bid is the price at which you would buy.

Spread

The difference between the bid price and the ask price of an option is called as a spread. The name spread is also referred to an options strategy that required the holding of two or more simultaneouspositions.

Different Order Types

There are different Types of order in the market. They are Market Order, Limit Order, Stop Loss/Sell Stop order, and Buy Stops order.

#1 Market Order

In market orders, you typically authorize the broker to sell or buy options at the best price available in the market.

#2 Limit Order

Limit Order is apretty useful type of order, as you need not necessarily get the best bid/ask spread prices due to fluctuations in the market. With the aid of limit orders, you can buy when the option falls to a certain price level or lower, or sell when the option increases above a certain price level.

#3 Stop Loss/Sell Stop order

Stop Loss/Sell Stop orders are used for limiting the losses from trades. This order is used for selling the options when it falls below a specific level. The stop loss is increased as per the increase in theprice of the options.

#4 Buy Stop order

Buy Stops order are used for purchasing options once it reaches or crosses a specific level of price. This is best used in scenarios wherein the options are expected to rise above certain resistance level or bounce back from certain support levels. There are two ways in which buy stop orders can be placed. They are: buy stop with limit and by stop with limit and stoploss.

There are also various time limits that can be set for trade orders. They are Good Till Cancelled (GTC), Day Only, Week Only, Fill or Kill, and All or None.

LEAPS (Long-term Equity AnticiPation Securities)

LEAPS constitute an importantpart of the options market. Typically, the standard options expire within a year's time. On the other hand, LEAPS have alonger expiration, up to even three years of time. The trading of LEAPS is done in the same manner as regular options. Typically, around 17% of the listed options are LEAPS. The securities on which the LEAPS should be listed is selected by each exchange based on the overall market interest.

The biggest advantage bestowed by LEAPS is flexibility for investors as the options have a good chance to move in the money within that time period.

Index Options

The puts and calls that are made on a stock index (eg: biotech industry, S&P 500 etc) are called as index options. These index options track entire sector or market as a whole.

Jordon Sykes

CHAPTER 3: SKILL #2 READING OPTIONS TABLE

Now that you are familiar with the various options terminologies, we can move onto the next skillset – reading an options table and understanding buying and selling of a put option as well as a call option.

The figure below shows the call option table of the stock AAPL in NASDAQ.

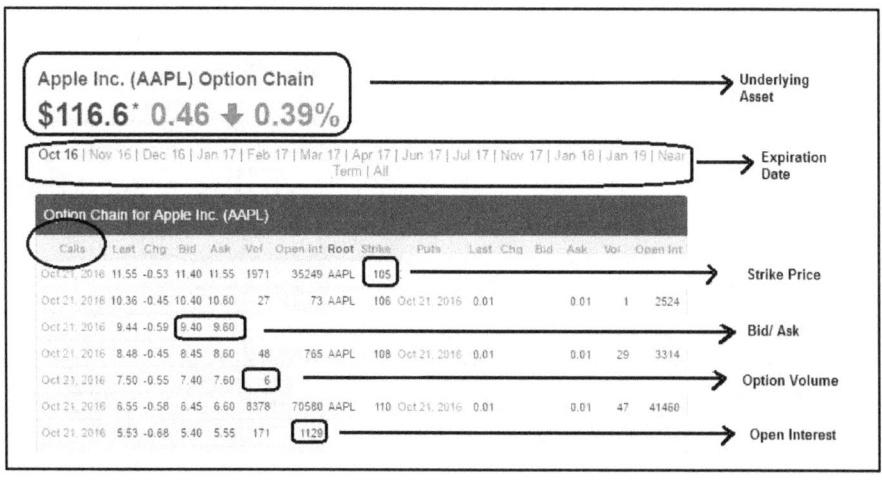

The figure below shows the put option table for Apple Inc.

Jordon Sykes

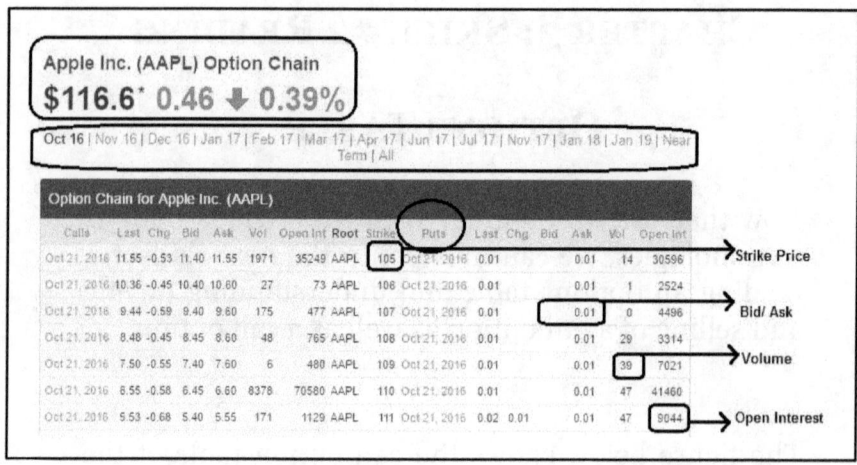

Options chain table is displayed in the Chicago Board Options Exchange (CBOE) as well.

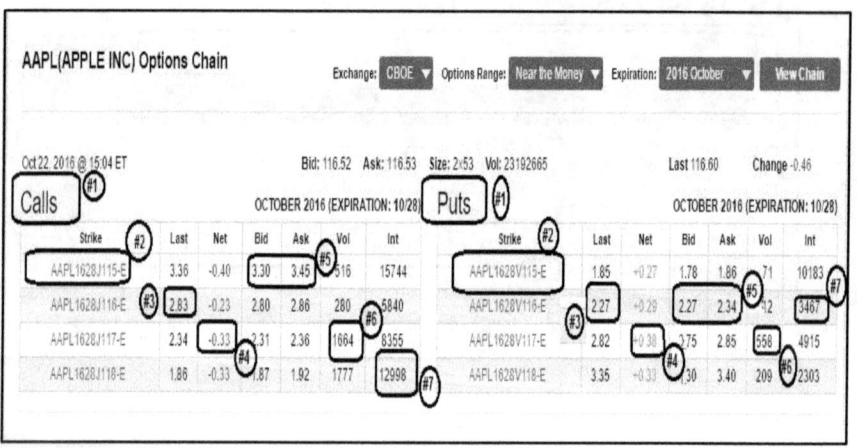

Let us now have a go at reading the various fields of options chain table

#1 Calls and Puts: Options are basically two kinds – Calls and Puts. Calls are same as going long and puts are same as going short in a stock.

#2 Expiration: The tables above shows the expiration on Friday, October 28th, 2016. It also shows the ***Strike Price***(ie, This is the price that an underlying stock can be bought or sold at.)

Symbols consist of the root symbol (AAPL) + the last two digits of the year (2016, so "16") + the day (28th of October so "28") + the month and option type code ("J" for October Call, "V" for October Put) + strike price code

#3 Last: This is the last price that someone has paid to purchase the options contract.

#4 Net/ Chg: This is the price change from previous day's closing price to today's current price.

#5 Bid/ Ask: The price at which you would buy or sell.

#6 Volume: The sum of contracts traded for the day

#7 Open Int: It is the number of open positions for an options series. It can also be defined as the number of open contracts in the current market.

Now that you are familiar with the various fields of anoptions table, let us delve deeper into calls and puts.

Buying and Selling call options

A call option can be bought as well as sold. Let us examine the difference between the two.

Buying call Options

When buying a Call Option it is typically known as along call. Basically, it is an option contract wherein the buyer (holder) has the right, notobligation, to buy a fixed quantity of a security at a specific price (also called as strike price) within its expiration date.

Usually buying call options is done when the investor expects the underlying stock to move upwards from the strike price within the expiration period. Buying a Call Option can provide technically **unlimited amount of profit** within its expiry date if the underlying security moves upwards. On the other hand, the **losses** incurred by purchasing a call option is **limited** to just the premium amount that was paid during the purchase.

This can be represented as shown in the figure below

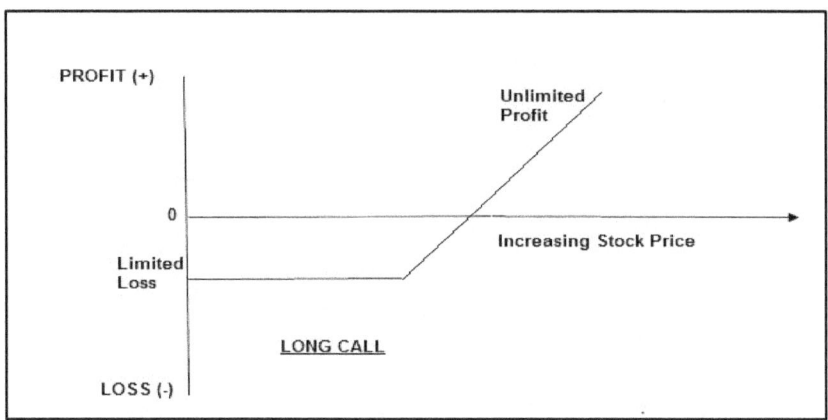

In summary, when buying a call option following are the potentials for profit and losses

Profit: Unlimited, it increases with the increase in the underlying stock price ***Loss***: Limited, the maximum loss that can happen is the amount of money paid as premium for buying the call

Steps to buy call option: First, decide on which strike price of the call option you want to buy, from the options table. Then place an order for 'Buy' for the call option for that selected strike price. Usually, if you place your buy price value equal to the 'Ask'

amount, your trade would get executed quicker. If you place an order for buying acall option with a price lesser than 'Ask' amount, the execution of the order might be slightly delayed.

Selling Call Options

In lieu of buying call options, you can also sell calls for making profits. This is known as writing calls.

Basically, it is an options contract wherein the call writer would have the obligation to sell the underlying security at the specified strike price if the option is exercised by the call buyer. The call option writer would receive a premium for taking on the risk relatedwith that obligation.

The call option sellers or writers typically sell call options with the expectation that the underlying stock would move downwards from the strikeprice within the expiration date. When the price moves downwards,the **option would expire worthless**. Hence, they would be able to pocket the **premiumamounts** and make **profits** this way. There are two ways to sell call options. They are Selling covered calls and Selling naked (uncovered) calls.

Selling callsis also called as a **short call**. Although this is riskier when compared to buying calls, it can also give you a tidy sum of profits if you do it properly.

This can be represented as shown in the figure below

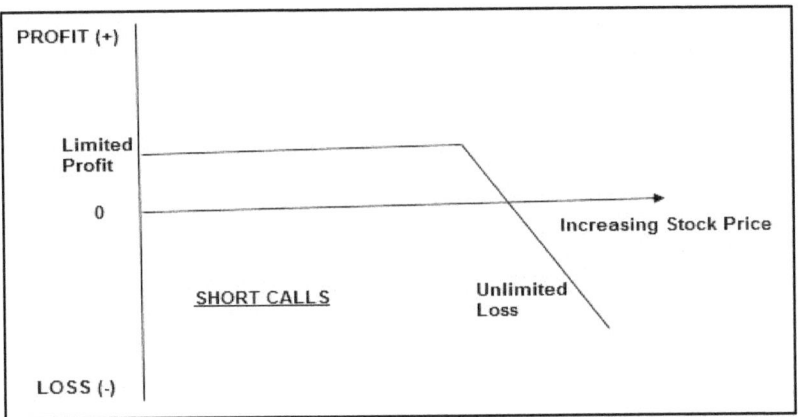

In summary, when selling a call option following are the potentials for profit and losses

Profit: Limited, the maximum profit that can be gained is the amount of money received aspremiumwhen selling the call.

Loss: Unlimited, the loss it increases with the increase in the underlying stock price

Steps to sell call option: First, decide on which strike price of the call option you want to sell, from the options table. Then place an order for 'Sell' for the call option for that selected strike price. Usually, if you place your sell price value equal to the 'Bid' amount, your trade would get executed quicker. If you place an order for selling acall option with a price higher than the 'Bid' amount, the execution of the order might be slightly delayed.

Buying and Selling Put options

A put option can be bought as well as sold. Let us examine the difference between the two.

Buying Put Options

When buying a put option, it is basically an option contract wherein the buyer (also known as the holder) has the right, not obligation to sell a specific quantity of the underlying stock or security at a definite strike price within the expiration period.

Usually buying put options is done when the investor expects the underlying stock to move downwardsfrom the strike price within the expiration period. Buying a Put Option can provide technically**substantial amount of profit** within its expiry date if the underlying security moves in adownward direction. On the other hand, the **losses** incurred by purchasing a put option is **limited** to just the premium amount that was paid during the purchase.

This can be represented as shown in the figure below

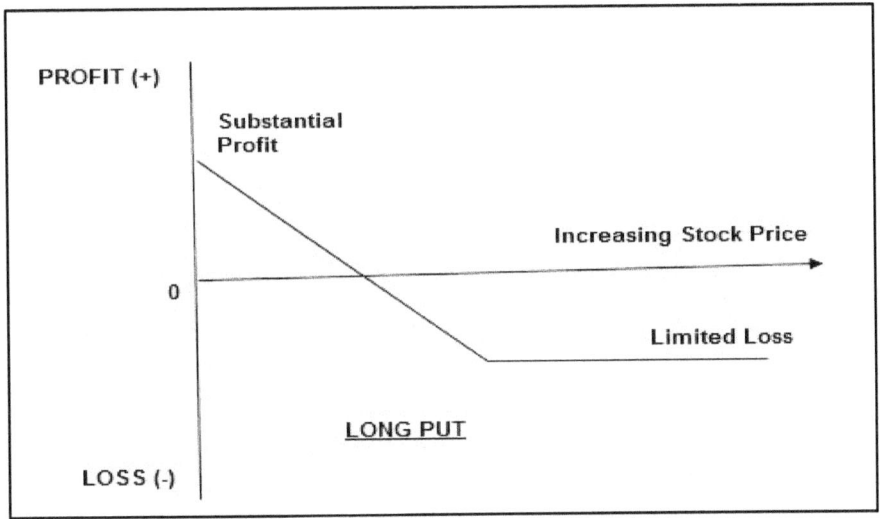

In summary, when buying a put option following are the potentials for profit and losses

Profit: Substantial, it increases with the decrease in the underlying stock price

Loss: Limited, the maximum loss that can happen is the amount of money paid as premium for buying the put

Steps to buy put option: First, decide on which strike price of the put option you want to buy, from the options table. Then place an order for 'Buy' for the put option for that selected strike price. Usually, if you place your buy price value equal to the 'Ask' amount, your trade would get executed quicker. If you place an order for buying aput option with a price lesser than 'Ask' amount, the execution of the order might be slightly delayed.

Selling Put Options

The writer or seller of a put option would have an obligation to buy the underlying stock at the strike price in case the option is exercised by the put buyer. The put option writer would receive a premium for taking on the risk relatedwith that obligation.

The put option sellers or writers typically sell put options with the expectation that the underlying stock would move upwards from the strike price within the expiration date. When the price moves upwards, the **option would expire worthless**. Hence, they would be able to pocket the **premiumamounts** and make **profits** this way. There are two ways to sell put options. They are Selling covered puts and Selling naked (uncovered) puts.

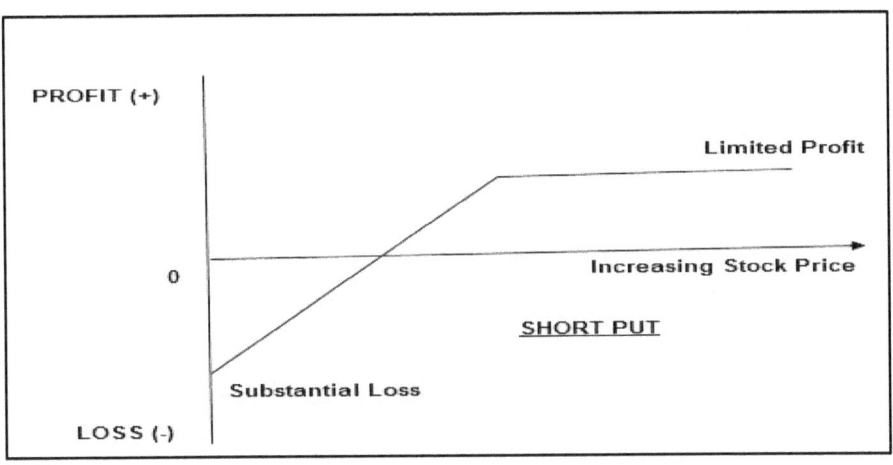

In summary, when selling a put option following are the potentials for profit and losses

Profit: Limited, the maximum profit that can be gained is the amount of money received as premiumwhen selling the put.

Loss: Substantial, the loss it increases with the decrease in the underlying stock price

Steps to sellput option: First, decide on which strike price of the put option you want to sell, from the options table. Then place an order for 'Sell' for the put option for that selected strike price. Usually, if you place your sell price value equal to the 'Bid' amount, your trade would get executed quicker. If you place an order for selling aput option with a price higher than the 'Bid' amount, the execution of the order might be slightly delayed.

Now that you have been familiarized with the Options table, buying puts, selling puts, buying calls, and selling calls; it is time to move on to the next important skillset – how to analyze options.

Chapter 4: Skill #3 Analyzing Options

Before you go ahead and actually buy or sell the calls or puts, it is important to perform an in-depth analysis of the Options. This would help in deciphering if the trade has a potential to be profitable.

Options can be analyzed using four methods. They are by using:

1. Technical Analysis
2. Open interest
3. Using option Greeks and volatility

In this chapter, you will learn about

- The basics of Technical Analysis and how to pick options based on the charts.
- Secrets for picking good options trades using Open Interest
- How to enter into a good option trade using option Greeks and volatility

#1 Technical Analysis

So, what exactly is technical analysis? In simple words, technical analysis comprises of chart reading in order to recognize the various chart patterns. They are theninterpreted in order to decisions regarding the timings for buying or selling the options as well as to make a trading plan.

Technical analysis is also hugely helpful in making the traders more disciplined as well as for money management.

There are basically two ways in which technical analysis can be performed. They are indicators and chart patterns.

- Chart patterns—they are basically patterns that give an indication of what is happening tothe price of the security.
- Indicators— indicators are basically mathematical algorithms. The indicators take into account the various aspects of underlying security'sprice movement and piece them together to create different kinds of ratios and analysis.

Using these ratios, the future price movement of the security can be guessed or predicted

The charts to be analyzed can either be the chart of the options or the chart of the underlying stock.

The following table lists out the important chart patterns, their important aspects, and whether they indicate a breakout or a reversal or both.

Chart Patterns – Quick Reference

Name	Figure	Important Points	Indicates
Support and resistance		Support is the price from which the stock bounces and moves upwards. Resistance is the price from which the stock bounces and moves downwards. After crossing a resistance, it can start to	Breakout or Reversal

		act as a support for the option For Trading: Bullish breakouts buy deep ITM call. Bearish breakouts buy deep ITM put.	
Double Tops	Top #1 Top #2 Price Moves Down Double Top Pattern	Double Top Pattern is a bearish pattern that indicates a trend reversal from bullish to a bearish bias. For Trading: Sell all trades on breakdown from the neckline. Ideal for buying puts.	Bearish Reversal

Double Bottoms	*Double Bottom Pattern chart*	Double Bottom Pattern is a bullish pattern that indicates a trend reversal from bearish to a bullish bias.	Bullish Reversal
		For Trading: Buy trades on breakout from the neckline. Ideal for buying calls.	
Triple Tops	*Triple Top Pattern chart*	Triple Top Pattern is a bearish pattern that indicates a trend reversal from bullish to a bearish bias.	Bearish Reversal
		For Trading: Sell all trades on breakdown from the neckline.	

		Ideal for buying puts.	
Triple Bottoms	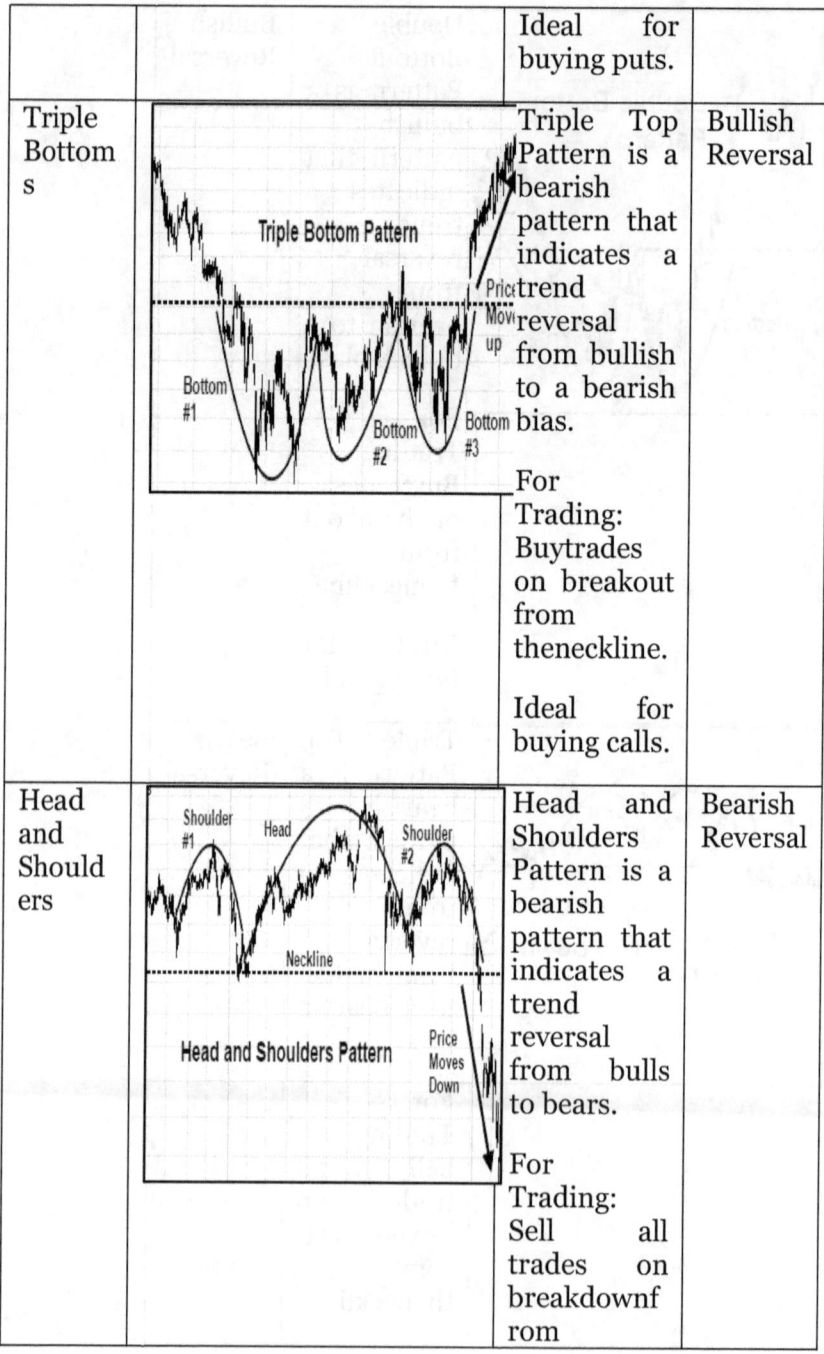	Triple Top Pattern is a bearish pattern that indicates a trend reversal from bullish to a bearish bias. For Trading: Buy trades on breakout from the neckline. Ideal for buying calls.	Bullish Reversal
Head and Shoulders		Head and Shoulders Pattern is a bearish pattern that indicates a trend reversal from bulls to bears. For Trading: Sell all trades on breakdown from	Bearish Reversal

		theneckline. Ideal for buying puts.	
Inverted Head and Shoulders		Inverted Head and Shoulders Pattern is a bullish pattern that indicates a trend reversal from bearish to a bullish bias. For Trading: Buytrades on breakout from theneckline. Ideal for buying calls.	Bullish Reversal
Pennants and Triangles		Triangle pattern is a continuation chart pattern. Price breaks out and moves in the same direction as the initial price trend	Breakout or Reversal

		For Trading: Buytrades on breakout. Ideal for buying calls.	
Bullish Flag	*(Continuation Chart Pattern — Flag Pattern, Price Moves Up)*	Bullish flag pattern is a continuation chart pattern. Price breaks out and moves in the same direction as the initial price trend. For Trading: Buytrades on breakout. Ideal for buying calls.	Upward Breakout
Cup and Handle	*(CUP AND HANDLE PATTERN)*	Cup and Handle pattern is a valued pattern which when confirmed indicates bullish breakouts. For	Upward Breakout

		Trading: Buytrades on breakout. Ideal for buying calls.	
Inverted Cup and Handle	INVERTED CUP AND HANDLE PATTERN	Inverted Cup and Handle pattern is a valued pattern which when confirmed indicate bearish breakouts. For Trading: Selltrades on breakout. Ideal for buying puts.	Downward Breakout
Doji	Doji	Doji is a neutral candlestick pattern indicating an indecision between the bulls and the bears. It serves as a reversal pattern if it is formed as	Reversal

		a 20 day high or low. For Trading: Bullish: buy deep ITM call Bearish: buy deep ITM put	

In addition to the above chart patterns, there are also few other chart patterns that indicate both reversals as well as breakout. Some of them are Fibonacci retracement and expansion, Trendlines, Elliott Wave, Gann, Gaps, and Volume spike.

Next, let us focus on the important indicators

Indicators – Quick Reference

Name of Indicator	Figure	Important Details	Signifies
MACD		When MACD line crosses above the signal	Reversal

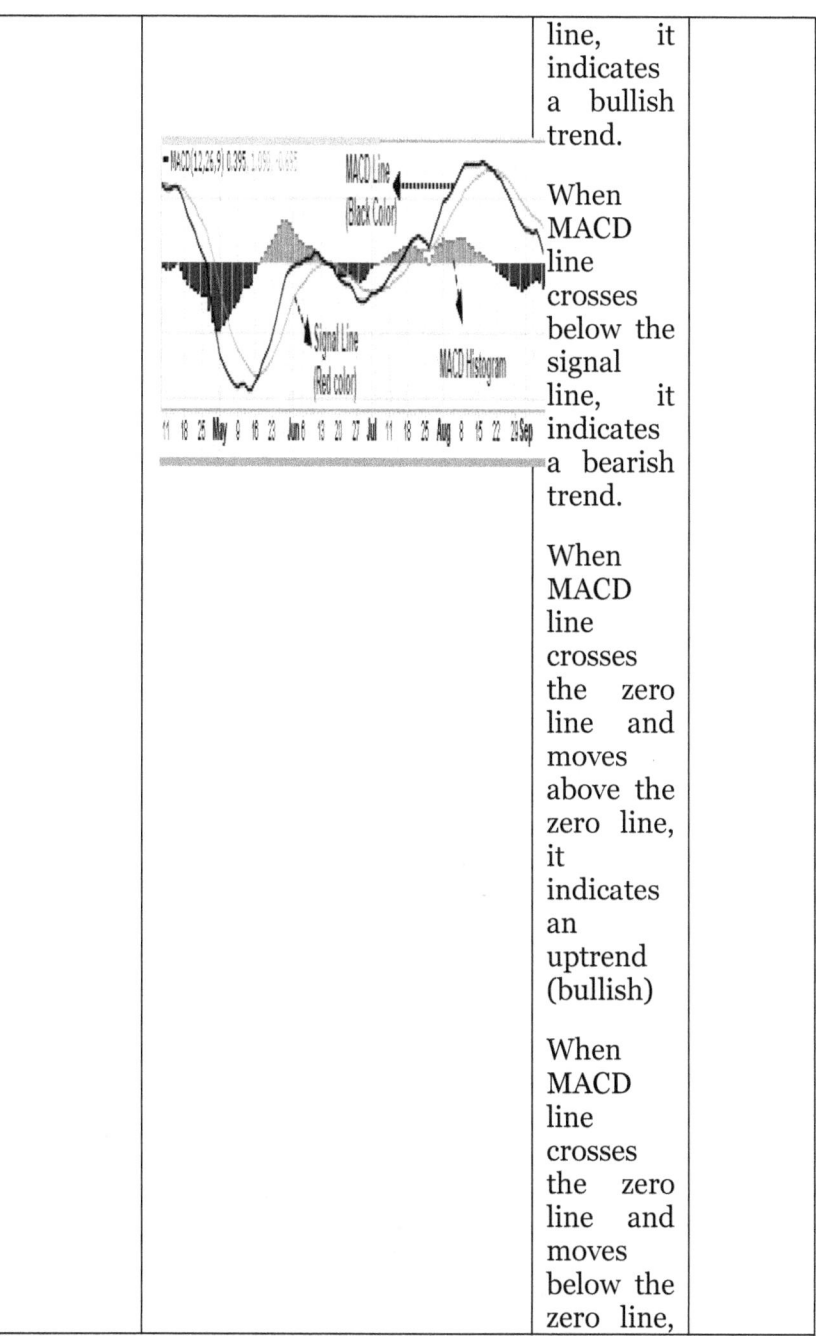

line, it indicates a bullish trend.

When MACD line crosses below the signal line, it indicates a bearish trend.

When MACD line crosses the zero line and moves above the zero line, it indicates an uptrend (bullish)

When MACD line crosses the zero line and moves below the zero line,

		it indicates a downtrend (bearish)	
Stochastics		When the value of Stochastics is above 80, it is considered as overbought. It is best to go for shorts or exit the stock at this point. When the value of Stochastics is below 20, it is considered as oversold. It is best to go for longs or enter the stock at this point.	Reversal
RSI		When the	Revers

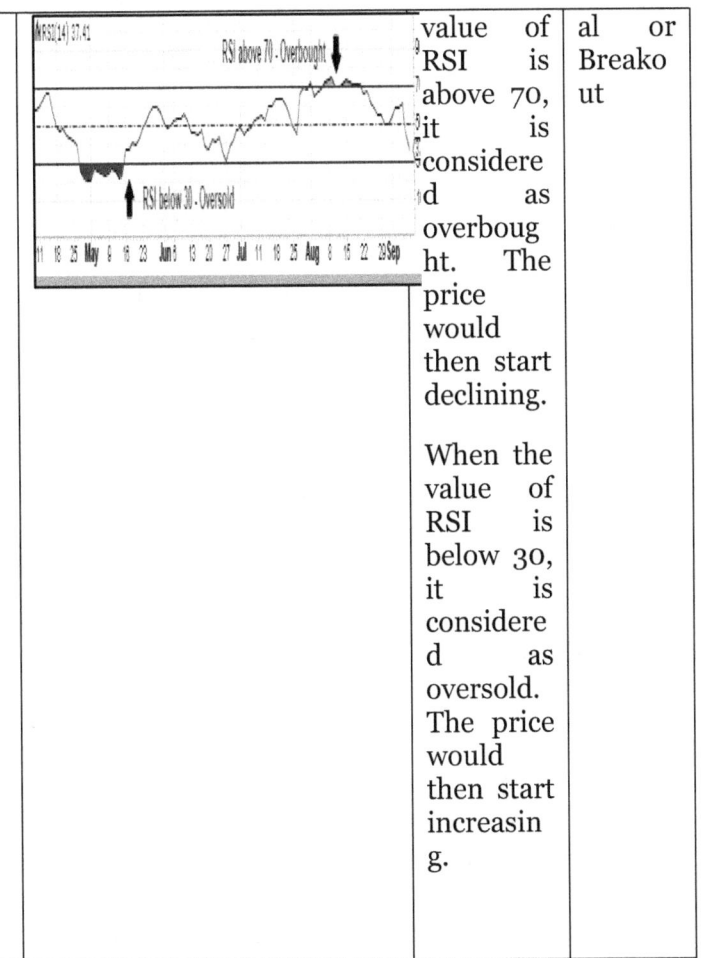	value of RSI is above 70, it is considered as overbought. The price would then start declining. When the value of RSI is below 30, it is considered as oversold. The price would then start increasing.	al or Breakout

#2 Open interest

The analysis of options is also done using open interests. As explained earlier, open interest is basically the number of options contracts that remain as open (also called as unexercised) at a given point in time.

An open contract is defined as a contract that has not beenexercisedor allowed to expire, or closed out.

- Whenever two parties enter into anew options contract, the open interest increases.
- Conversely, in case the existing contract is liquidated, the open interest decreases.

In short, open interest is a measure of the activity of the underlying security or a measure of its liquidity.

So how does the value of open interest help in analyzing options?

- Whenever there is an increase in the open interest along with a rise in price, it indicates that the existing trend is strong and the underlying stock would continue to follow the current direction of stock, indicating bullishness.
- Whenever there is a decrease in price and a falling openInterest, it is considered to be a sign of areversal of the existing trend. Hence, this is a sign of bullishness.
- Whenever there is an increase in open interest with a decrease in price, it indicates bearishness.

- Whenever there is a decrease in open interest and an increase in price, it is a sign of bearishness.

Hence, the trading can be done according to the trend that is expected to occur. The table below shows what type of trades can be taken based on open interest and price.

Open Interest	Price	Bullish or Bearish	Trades
Increase	Increase	Bullish	Buy Calls/ Any bullish Option Strategies
Increase	Decrease	Bearish	Buy Puts/ Any bearish Option Strategies
Decrease	Increase	Bearish Reversal	Buy Puts/ Any bearish Option Strategies
Decrease	Decrease	Bullish Reversal	Buy Calls/ Any bullish Option Strategies

#3 Using option Greeks and volatility

The options can also be analyzed based on the implied volatility of the underlying stock.

Whenever the volatility is low, the time premium is relatively lesser and the price would also be lower. Hence, it is best to buy options when volatility is low. This way, you will be able to exit the trade with good profits once the volatility increases and the price get inflated.

On the other hand, a high volatility implies that the time premium is higher and the price would be higher. Hence, the subsequent decline of volatility would deflate the option price. In such a scenario, it is best to sell options during high volatility and then cover later when the volatility becomes lower.

The trading strategy to be followed is represented as shown in the figure below

Volatility	Option Price	Trading
High	High	Write Options
Low	Low	Buy Options

Now that you have understood the various methods of options analysis, you can move on tolearn the various option strategies for making profits in various scenarios. This is covered in detail in the next chapter.

Chapter 5: Skill #4 Option Strategies

Following are the most important options strategies that are ideal for any novice investors.

- Long Call Strategy
- Long Put Strategy
- Covered Call Strategy
- Synthetic CallStrategy
- Synthetic PutStrategy

Here, a quick overview of these simple and easy to follow strategies are provided, for reference.

Strategy #1: Long Call

Objective and Rationale: Buy the call with the expectation that the price of the underlying security would increase.

Summary: Buy Calls

Strategy Overview

Market direction expected	Bullish
Intended for	Capital Gains
Transaction Type	Net Debit (paying for call option)

Risk Profile

Maximum Risk	Call premium
Maximum Reward	Unlimited
Breakeven Price	Call strike price + call premium

Strategy #2: Long Put

Objective and Rationale: Buy the put with the expectation that the price of the underlying security would decrease.

Summary: Buy Puts

Strategy Overview

Market direction expected	Bearish
Intended for	Capital Gains
Transaction Type	Net Debit (paying for put option)

Risk Profile

Maximum Risk	Put premium
Maximum Reward	Substantial
Breakeven Price	Put strike price - put premium

Strategy #3: Covered Call

Objective and Rationale: This strategy is intended for the stocks that you already own. The idea here is to sell an Out of the Money call option on the stock that you own and pocket the premium. Then, there could be three potential outcomes for this:

- If the stock increases above the strike price, the stock would be sold as it will be exercised. However, you would still make a profit.

- If there is no change in the stock price until the expiration date, you can just pocket the collected premium for the call you sold.

- If the stock decreases, you would still have the cushion of the call premium that was collected.

You can also sell an In the Money or At the Money call of the stock you own if you believe that the stock is going to move down or sideways. Usually, the premium value would be higher, as will the likelihood of exercise.

Summary: Buy Stock and Sell OTM Call

Strategy Overview

Market direction expected	Neutral to Bullish
Intended for	Income
Transaction Type	Net Debit (paying for the stock and only getting a small premium for the sold call options.)

Risk Profile

Maximum Risk	Stock price paid - call premium
Maximum Reward	Substantial
Breakeven Price	Call premium + (Call strike - stock price paid)

Strategy #4: Synthetic Call

Objective and Rationale: This strategy is intended for protecting the stocks that you already own. The idea here is to insure against a potential loss by buying an At The Money or slightly On The Money (lower strike) put.

In case the stock price breaks down, the value of long put will increase and counter the loss in theprice of the long stock position.

Summary: Buy Stock and Buy ATM/OTM Put

Strategy Overview

Market direction expected	conservatively bullish
Intended for	Capital Gain
Transaction Type	Net Debit (buying both the stock and the put.)

Risk Profile

Maximum Risk	Stock price - put premium - put strike price]
Maximum Reward	Unlimited
Breakeven Price	Strike price - put premium - stock price - put strike price

Strategy #5: Synthetic Put

Objective and Rationale: This strategy is actually the opposite of Synthetic Call. In this strategy, first, you short the stock and then buy an At The Money or slightlyOn The Money(higher strike) call. In case the stock price breaks out and increase in value, the value of long call will increase and counter the loss in theprice of the short stock position.

Summary: Sell Stock and Buy ATM/OTM Call

Strategy Overview

Market direction expected	Bearish
Intended for	Capital Gain
Transaction Type	Net Credit

Risk Profile

Maximum Risk	Call strike price - stock price - call premium
Maximum Reward	Lowest Stock price - call premium
Breakeven Price	Stock price - call premium

Another important strategy that you must be aware of is called as spreads.

What is a spread?

A Spreadis basically an options strategy which consists of two transactions or trades. They are typically executed at thesame time.

Usually, you would need to purchase an option and write another option on the same underlying stock orindex. The only difference between these identical options would be in a single element like strike price or expirationdate.

Note: Whenever you **buy an option**, it is called as a**long leg**. Whenever you **write an option**, it is called as a**short leg**.

When the two options differ by strike price, it is called as a **vertical spread**. It is of four types - the bull put, the bull call, thebear put, and the bear call. Here is a quick explanation of each of the four vertical spreads

- ***Bull Put:*** Buy Put at lowerstrike, Write Put at higherstrike
- ***Bull Call:*** Buy Call at lowerstrike, Write Call at higherstrike

- ***Bear Put:*** Buy Put at higherstrike, Write Put at lowerstrike

- ***BearCall:*** Buy Call at higherstrike, Write Call at lowerstrike

When the two options differ by expiration date, it is called as a **calendar spread**. A calendar spread is usually a neutral strategy.

When you write or purchase both a put as well as a call on an underlying stock or index with thesame strike price as well as same expiration date, it is called as a **straddle.**

When you write or purchase both a put as well as a call on an underlying stock or index with thesame expiration date, but a different Out of The Money strike price, it is called as **strangle**.

Another spread strategy that is intended toprotect unrealized profits on thestock youalready own is called as a **collar or Fence**. Here, you basically buy a protectiveput on your long stock and compensatethe money you spent on that put by writing a call that iscovered by your long stock position.

Now, every novice trader would have a different risk tolerance level as well as objectives for taking options.

The tables below gives a quick summary of the various basic options strategies and where they can be applied depending on the objective of the options trader.

There can be three basic objectives

a. To receive income or speculate

b. To protect the portfolio profit or improve the purchase price

c. To make profit from market/ sector move

Case (A): If the objective of the Options Trader is to **receive income or speculate**, following are the options trading strategies based on your market expectation as well as risk tolerance level.

Your Expectation about the market	Risk Tolerance	Ideal Strategy
Very Bullish	Low	Buy OTM calls
Bullish	Low	Buy Calls

Moderate Bullish	Low	Open Bull Call Spread
Bullish/ Neutral	Low	Open Bull Put Spread
Bearish/ Neutral	Low	Open Bear Call Spread
Moderate Bearish	Low	Open Bear Put Spread
Bearish	Low	Buy Puts
Very Bearish	Low	Buy OTM puts
Moderate Bullish/ Neutral	Moderate	Write covered calls on stocks of your portfolio
Bullish/ Neutral	High	Write naked Puts
Bearish/ Neutral	Very High	Write naked Calls

Case (B): If the objective of the Options Trader is to **protect the portfolio profit or improve the purchase price**, the following are the options trading strategies based on your market expectation as well as risk tolerance level.

Your Expectation about the market	Risk Tolerance	**Ideal Strategy**
Neutral/ slightly Bullish	Low	Buy calls to lock in purchase price

Neutral/ Bullish	Low	Buy-write to lower your net price paid
Neutral/ Bullish (long term)	Low	Write puts to lower your net price paid
Neutral/ Moderately Bearish	Low	Open a collar to lock in potential gains
Very Bearish/ Bullish (long term)	Low	Buy puts
Bearish/ Bullish (long term)	Low	Buy out-of-the-money puts

Case (C): If the objective of the Options Trader is to **make profits from a sector or market move**, the following are the options trading strategies based on your market expectation as well as risk tolerance level.

Your Expectation about the market	Risk Tolerance	Ideal Strategy
Bullish	Low	Buy Index calls
Bearish	Low	Buy Index Puts
Neutral/ Bullish	Very High	Write Index Puts
Neutral/ Bearish	Very High	Write Index Calls

There are also option strategies that are ideal for intermediate traders, advanced traders and expert traders. Below are the list of such strategies according to the level of expertise of the trader. However, explaining each strategy is not within the scope of this book.

The option strategies that are ideal for **Intermediate traders** are:

- Bear Call Spread
- Bull Put Spread
- Bear Call Spread
- Bull Put Spread
- Calendar Call
- Collar
- Diagonal Call
- Long Call Butterfly
- Long Iron Butterfly
- Long Iron Condor
- Long Put Butterfly
- Short (Naked) Put

- Short Call Butterfly
- Short Put Butterfly
- Straddle
- Strangle

The option strategies that are ideal for **Advanced traders** are:

- Bear Call Ladder
- Bear Put Ladder
- Bull Call Ladder
- Bull Put Ladder
- Calendar Put
- Call Ratio Backspread
- Covered Put
- Covered Short Straddle
- Covered Short Strangle
- Diagonal Put
- Long Call Condor
- Long Put Condor
- Short (Naked) Call

- Put Ratio Backspread
- Short Call Condor
- Short Iron Butterfly
- Short Iron Condor
- Short Put Condor
- Short Straddle
- Short Strangle

The option strategies that are ideal for **Expert traders** are:

- Guts
- Long Box
- Long Call Synthetic Straddle
- Long Combo
- Long Put Synthetic Straddle
- Long Synthetic Future
- Modified Call Butterfly
- Modified Put Butterfly
- Ratio Call Spread
- Ratio Put Spread

- Short Call Synthetic Straddle
- Short Combo
- Short Guts

Options strategies can be categorized based on the direction of the market.

Following are the various bullish, bearish and neutral options strategies

Bullish Strategies	Bearish Strategies	Neutral Strategies
<ul><li>Bear Call Ladder</li><li>Bull Call Spread</li><li>Bull Put Spread</li><li>Calendar Call</li><li>Calendar Put</li><li>Call Ratio Backsprea</li></ul>	<ul><li>Bear Call Spread</li><li>Bear Put Spread</li><li>Bull Put Ladder</li><li>Covered Put</li><li>Long Put</li><li>Short (Naked) Call</li></ul>	<ul><li>Bear Put Ladder</li><li>Bull Call Ladder</li><li>Guts</li><li>Long Box</li><li>Long Call Butterfly</li><li>Long Call</li></ul>

- d - Collar - **Covered Call** - Covered Short Straddle - Covered Short Strangle - Diagonal Call - Diagonal Put - Long Call - Long Combo - Long Synthetic Future - Modified Call Butterfly - Modified Put Butterfly - Short (Naked)	- Put Ratio Backspread - Ratio Call Spread - Short Combo - Short Synthetic Future - Strip - **Synthetic Put**	- Condor - Long Call Synthetic Straddle - Long Iron Butterfly - Long Iron Condor - Long Put Butterfly - Long Put Condor - Long Put Synthetic Straddle - Short Call Butterfly - Short Call Condor

Put • Ratio Put Spread • Strap • **_Synthetic Call_**		• Short Call Synthetic Straddle • Short Guts • Short Iron Butterfly • Short Iron Condor • Short Put Butterfly • Short Put Condor • Short Put Synthetic Straddle • Short Straddle • Short Strangle • Straddle

		• Strangle

Options strategies can also be categorized based on High and Low Volatility strategies. They are as follows

High Volatility Strategies	Low Volatility Strategies
• Bear Call Ladder	• Bear Call Ladder
• Bull Put Ladder	• Bull Call Ladder
• Calendar Call	• Long Call Butterfly
• Call Ratio Backspread	• Long Call Condor
• Collar	• Long Iron Butterfly
• Diagonal Call	• Long Iron Condor
• Guts	• Long Put Butterfly
• Long Box	• Long Put Condor
• Long Call Synthetic Straddle	• Modified Call Butterfly
• Long Put Synthetic Straddle	• Modified Put Butterfly
• Put Ratio Backspread	• Ratio Call Spread
• Short Call Butterfly	• Ratio Put Spread
	• Short Call Synthetic Straddle

• Short Call Condor • Short Iron Butterfly • Short Iron Condor • Short Put Butterfly • Short Put Condor • Straddle • Strangle • Strap • Strip	• Short Guts • Short Put Synthetic Straddle • Short Straddle • Short Strangle

Options strategies are also available for obtaining regular income as well as for Capital Gain.

Strategies for Regular Income	Strategies for Capital Gain
• Bear Call Spread • Bear Put Ladder • Bull Call Ladder • Bull Put Spread • Calendar Call • Calendar Put • **Covered Call**	• Bear Call Ladder • Bear Put Spread • Bull Call Spread • Bull Put Ladder • Call Ratio Backspread • Collar

- Covered Put
- Covered Short Straddle
- Covered Short Strangle
- Diagonal Call
- Diagonal Put
- Long Iron Butterfly
- Long Iron Condor
- Short (Naked) Call
- Short (Naked) Put
- Ratio Call Spread
- Ratio Put Spread
- Short Guts
- Short Put Synthetic Straddle
- Short Straddle
- Short Strangle

- Guts
- Long Box
- Long Call
- Long Call Butterfly
- Long Call Condor
- Long Call Synthetic Straddle
- Long Combo
- Long Put
- Long Put Butterfly
- Long Put Condor
- Long Put Synthetic Straddle
- Long Synthetic Future
- Modified Call Butterfly
- Modified Put Butterfly
- Put Ratio Backspread
- Short Call Butterfly
- Short Call Condor
- Short Call Synthetic

	Straddle
	• Short Combo
	• Short Iron Butterfly
	• Short Iron Condor
	• Short Put Butterfly
	• Short Put Condor
	• Short Synthetic Future
	• Straddle
	• Strangle
	• Strap
	• Strip
	• **Synthetic Call**
	• **Synthetic Put**

Now that you have familiarized yourself with the fundamental skills for dominating options trading, it is time to start putting the things you have learnt into practice. For that, it is ideal to start with a demo account and see how you fare on the options trading. It can be used to narrow down to a style of options trading that works for you. Once you have gained the confidence and start making consistent profits in the demo trading, you can start options trading with actual money.

Bonus Chapter: Secrets for Successful Options Trading

In this bonus section, I will be disclosing some of the secrets forOptions Trading that has helped me maximize profits over the years.

1. Have an exit strategy in place: Planning the proper exit is pivotal for gaining maximum profits from options. It would also help in minimizing losses. Hence, it is always important to establish how you will exit if your option is OTM, ITM, or ATM even before you take a trade.

This is best explained using an example.

Assume that you currently hold an 'ABC' 80 call that had cost you $200. Then, when deciding the exit, you will have to factor in the $2 per share that was spent on the option.

2. When the volatility is low, look to buy options as there is a good chance of the volatility to increase resulting in increased premium.

3. When the volatility is high, look to sell options as there is a good chance of the volatility cooling down and thereby

decreasing the premiums. This is especially ideal to dobefore important events like GDP data, quarterly results etc. Just before the event, the volatility would be on the higher side. Selling options right before the event is a good strategy.

4. To limit the risk, it is preferable to buy options. Selling an option can result in unlimited losses. Having said that, selling deep out of the money options a few days before the expiry is a safe method to generate some monthly income.

5. It is very important to choose the right strike price before buying or selling an option. The strike price has to be decided based on thefactors like thecurrent market price of the underlying stock, the options Greek Delta, the number of days left for the expiry etc. Let us assume that the stock ABC has a current market price of 100. Also, let us assume that you are bullish on this stock and looking to buy a call option. So, the strike price can be selected after considering the following.

   a. If the number of days to expiry is more than 30, then it would be better to go for deep out of the money calls. Deep OTM calls have been shown to move the most when there is ample time to the expiry and the underlying stock surges. However, while selecting a deep OTM option, do make sure to select a strike price with delta greater than or equal to 0.2. If the delta is less than 0.2, there is a good chance that the stock might expire worthless.

b. If the number of days to expiry is less than 30 but more than 15, then it would be better to go for slight out of the money calls. It has been shown from past data that slight OTM calls moves the most, in this particular scenario. However, while selecting a slight out of the money call option, do make sure to select a strike with adelta of 0.4 or above. If the delta is less than 0.4, there is a good chance that the stock might expire worthless, as there is only less than one month to expiry.

c. If the number of days to expiry is less than 15, ATM or At the Money calls are seen to perform the best. Since the number of days to expiry is less, it would be better to go for a strike price very close to the current market price of the underlying stock. At the moneycallswould have a delta of 0.5.

d. If the expiry is just a few days away, then it would be better to go for deep

'In the money' calls. This would be very similar to taking a futures contract as the call option would move in conjunction with the price of the underlying stock. The delta of a deep ITM option would be close to 1. This means that for every $1 movement in the stock, the call option would also move by the same amount.

6. Option contracts can also be used in lieu of a futures contract. Here is how. The delta of afutures contract is 1, which essentially means the futures contract moves by the same amount as the underlying stock. So, in order to replace a futures contract, we would need to take 'N' number of options contract so that the sum of the delta equals 1. For example, a deep OTM call might have a delta of 0.2. So, in order for this to work like a futures contract, you can get 5 lots of the deep OTM call, so that the total delta equals 1. So, 5 lots of deep OTM call option of delta 0.2 would move by the same amount as the underlying stock.

7. Options can be used to hedge the long-term portfolio. In order to protect our long-term portfolio, buy Put options (the strategies for this are covered in the earlier section). This can protect your portfolio from a lot of unforeseen events like arecession, war and other global events can cause the stock market to crash.

8. Options can be used to generate monthly income. Covered calls can be written using the stocks already in the portfolio to generate a monthly income. Deep OTM calls can be written every month, to generate 1 or 2 %. The only downside to this is if the stock moves up more than anticipated. In that case, the stock in our portfolio would have to be exercised or sold off. Even so, you are still selling ata profit.

9. Even though buying options limits the risk, options expire worthlessmore often than not. As the saying goes, amateurs buy options and experts sell options. Though this is not entirely true, it is a little hard to make money by buying options. As discussed earlier, choosing the right strike price is very important. Also, one has to very careful while selling options as the risk is unlimited.

10. Like stocks, proper money management rules are very important while trading in options as well. Never risk more than 5 % of your trading capital on a single trade. A stop loss should be decided in advance and entered into the system as soon as the trade is live. Though Options are powerful wealth creating instruments, they also have a huge risk associated with it. So, it is very important to follow all the money management rules and not to over trade. If you are a beginner it is

not advisable to sell options as they carry unlimited risk. Another classic mistake is purchasing deep OTM calls as they cost less and they eventually expire worthlesslyin most cases.

Conclusion

Thank you again for downloading this book!

I hope this book was able to help you gain all the fundamental skills required to dominate Options Trading.

The next step is to apply the strategies and techniques mentioned in the book in real life for becoming asuccessful Options Trader.By religiously following important analysis and strategies listed in the book, your Options Trading is guaranteed to give you humongous financialbenefits.

Finally, if you enjoyed this book, then I'd like to ask you for a favor, would you be kind enough to leave a review for this book on Amazon? It'd be greatly appreciated!

Click here to leave a review for this book on Amazon!

Thank you and good luck!

Jordon Sykes

Options Trading: Fundamental Skills To Dominate Options Trading

Points you will learn

This book contains complex Fundamental as well as Technical concepts explained in a simple, easy to follow manner. Every section is described in detail with the aid of examples, charts, tables, or graphs. This book will help you

- Understand the fundamental skills required to become a Options Trader
- Identify the key Jargons and terms
- Learn how to analyze options
- Understand the important Options strategies that can help in making money

Benefits of reading the book

Equipped with the knowledge gained from this book, your overall outlook towards Options trading is guaranteed to become more positive as well as open.

The contents of this book are guaranteed to be extremely helpful for novice Options Traders as well as for the Veterans of the field. For the newbies, this book can be used as an important single point reference on the Options Trading Fundamental Skills. For the experts, this book would serve as a great refresher course.

If you wish to change your OptionsTrading for better by having a thorough understanding about all the required Fundamental Skills, we have got it covered!

www.ingramcontent.com/pod-product-compliance
Lightning Source LLC
Chambersburg PA
CBHW061149180526
45170CB00002B/692